It Began...
so innocently

PAUL GIVENS

ISBN: 0615642322
ISBN-13: 9780615642321

DEDICATION

To Mom.
To my friends.
My inspiration comes from the chapters of life we've written together.

CONTENTS

1   <u>It Began So Innocently</u>   1

Certainty   2

Bus   3

Fiction   4

Quixotic   5

Never   6

Balcony   7

More   8

Hopeful   9

Release   10

White Walls   11

Flight   12

Mirror   13

2   <u>Then Thought Crept In</u>   15

    Best Days   16

    Devices   18

    Where   19

    Blue   20

    Gone   22

    Conform   23

    Scars   24

    Samantha   25

    Hell   26

    War   27

3   <u>But Love Won Me Over</u>   30

    Destination   31

    Space   32

    Rush   33

    Eager   34

Hope	35
Key	37
She	39
Supernova	40

4   <u>Until My Mind Was Opened</u>   42

Sad Song	43
No Man's Land	45
E	47
Bend	48
Resistance	49
Beautiful	50
Inspired?	51
July	52
Wake	53
Undone	54
Chelsea	55

Cut   57

Close   58

Perfect   59

5   <u>To All That Was</u>   60

    For You   61

    Habit   62

    Without   63

    Sometimes   64

    Sifting   65

    Time   66

    Save   67

    Drive   68

6 <u>And All That Wasn't</u>   70

   Fire   71

   Lovely   72

   Two Years   73

   Bagel   75

   Inside   77

   You   78

   Walk   80

   Friend   82

   Together   83

   It Began   84

PAUL GIVENS

1
IT BEGAN SO INNOCENTLY

If today never ends
and tomorrow never comes
forever would be nice

Certainty

To hell with Certainty
Who needs it
The highest kites
don't fly with strings
The fastest runners
don't run in lanes
It's a matter of preference
Big risk
equals big reward
In order to land in a good place
you must first jump
In order to be something
you must refuse to be nothing

Maybe I'm still drunk from last night
Maybe I'm just in a good place
'Cause I'm finally feeling alive
for the first time
in a long time
And I'm catching the next flight to nowhere
hoping to land somewhere
So if I see you on the other side
I'll know your feet left the ground
and hopefully you've found
what you're looking for

Bus

She inspired me
more than she'll ever know
My heart burns warm
and it shows
as I think these thoughts
and write these words
She seeks out the good
in the worst of us
She builds her karma
while sitting on a bus
She looks at the lady in back
with the screaming kid
squirming on her lap
She listens to the man
with the Blackberry in hand
The words he speaks
conflict with her beliefs
But to each his own she thinks
The wheels turn
on the bus
and in her mind
She longs to meet
she longs to find
someone who'll talk shop
talk life
talk love
and everything in between
She sits in the back
of a metro transit bus
She looks for conversation
She looks for life
She looks for the best
in the worst of us

Fiction

A wave of love
rolling on the shore
A page of fiction
turning into truth at your door
So often,
we outrun the storms
meant to make us strong
Sometimes we escape
the most honest parts of our fate
I fear that running
rarely leads to something

There's beauty in the calm
passion in the storm
And as quickly as it begins
it will end
So beautiful
are the fruits of labor
born from the struggle
When the clear skies overflow with rain
the power of tomorrow
can ease the pain
The dawn of a new day
will breathe the winds of change

Quixotic

The odds I can take
The mold I can break
Nothing lasts forever
Nothing is Never!
Pick up
what you can't put down
Climb
what you can't get around
Trust what's hidden
Build the vision
It's about to crack
It's about to fall
The world needs a hero
to inspire us all
Are you gonna sit on the side
or join in the fight
die for tomorrow
or live for tonight

Never

Life's a walk in the sand
the silent bond
between a woman and man
The throw of a baseball
from one man to the next
the calm of two women
not putting each other to the test

The one who brings the most happiness
can bring the most pain
but it's a chance you gotta take
to feel the warmth of love's flames
Never refrain
from the chance to gain
a friend
or a lover
Life's a gift
a chance to uplift
a heart overwhelming a fist
a beautiful moment
your soul
finding a reason to exist

Balcony

The air is warm
and in the distance
the glow of the sunset
I sit,
we sit
and energize our minds
with the voices flowing
through the twilight of stars and sky
I've never written a word on my own
The breeze fills the blanks
with a light I could never see
And the people who said goodbye
come back to help me
So from now
to the next
it's my soul and mind they protect
There's no sleep
no rest
just a seat on the balcony
with the stars and the souls
that guide and watch over me

P.S.

I got the call
on the night of September 7th
4 days before New York
My tower fell that night
Tuesday was just Novocain for the pain
And I miss her
but she's still here
pushing me in the right direction
Me and you got a place in the heavens
Me and you got a place in the sun

More

I drive through the hills
through the twists and turns
though I have it all
my heart still yearns
I drive through the hills
and my destination draws near
Happiness and peace
are what I find here

A forest of green
soothes the beast in me
I need the stars at night
to help me believe
I've seen the big city
and all the flashing lights
Can't talk to the strangers
Gotta keep it on the inside

I sit with my friends
We enjoy life and all its gifts
and on our old times
we reminisce
I'm at peace
for love surrounds me
and I can just let go
because they love me
for me

Hopeful

I'm hopeful,
but not holding my breath
Guess it's my pessimism
messin' with my optimism
I'm hopeful,
but as the saying goes
Sometimes you gotta let it go
to see if it comes back home
So,
I'll try to relax
and hope my good karma comes back
I'm hopeful,
but not holding my breath
hopefully,
anticipating the next

Release

It's so amazing
so tender
so sweet
This warm wind blows
through my fingers then up my arm
And when the moment seems gone
I feel yet another
And when she touches me
I know,
I know I'm home
Summer comes along
and so it is
another moment in my life
I'll yearn to relive
With memories so fond
my heart lingers along
Warm in my soul
the dark is lifted
Alone in my mind
I dance and I smile
Without a word or thought
I release,
and let my worries float away

White Walls

Hardwood floors
Bronze-knobbed doors
A one-room flat in the Hillcrest District
Alone,
in a world of my own
My last days
in a place I once called home
Soon I'll wave goodbye
to the warm sand
of an all-too-foreign land
White walls
and a blow-up mattress
I'll pen a song or two
to mark the end of my youth
A dream that lived and died
only survives in my mind

I lay still
in my place of solitude
This apartment
embarks on a journey of its own
soon to be torn down
for what they call progress
Kind of fitting
to say goodbye
and have nothing to come back to
White walls
hardwood floors
bronze-knobbed doors
a little less
felt like a whole lot more

Flight

Out of sight
Over the hills
and into the night
On the runway
taking flight
Heading into the future
without a fight
Been to the past
no need to look back
Living on a wire
Looking for something to inspire,
me
Free to be,
independent
Free to believe
Free to love
Free to grieve
All that's gone
makes room for what's to come
My past and my present
add to my future sum
No regrets
I'm livin' to let
fate crunch the numbers

Mirror

He was dark
like a starless night
yet cast a brilliant
fantastic light
A boy whispered in his ear
"you have a pretty smile"
And this boy was right
A beautiful smile shown across his face
and no amount of pain
could ever take it away
He was truth in soul
out of,
yet somehow in control

His face
like a stern autumn breeze
carved the air
with a subtlety and ease
Through the eyes
seep the deepest of truths
When she looked into his eyes
she knew
"Your mother is your life"
This intuitive girl was right
His mother was his guiding light
his moral insight
the calming voice
through the darkest of nights
The mirror
that helped me see
that the brightest light
was the one she lit
inside of me

2
THEN THOUGHT CREPT IN

I wage war against myself,
because I've never known peace
I bathe in frustration,
because I've never been clean

Best Days

She plays the guitar
on a stage filled with lights
bridging the gap
between wrong and right
She picks and she strums
She looks into the crowd
and tries to connect with someone
She tells the stories
she read the night before
in the pages of a paper
people her age rarely explore
She talks of guns and bombs
while the crowd cheers
and sings along
They're not really listening
to the words they're repeating
She fears the worst
'cause it's all she sees
a bunch of zombies
jumping at her feet
When did we
get so fuckin' lame

She plays the guitar
on a stage filled with lights
bridging the gap
between day and night
She'd always dreamed
of making it big
She'd always wanted
to be the shit
But being the shit,
she's so over it
The stage is the star
She's just a shiny new car

passing by
She sings
and the people jump around
They get up
as she gets down
The lights grow dim
and the glitter fades
'cause she realizes
this country
has seen her best days

Devices

The world spins out of control
but death ain't got shit on me
I've got an iPhone
and a hi-def tv
The devices of sacrifice
Reality shows are about as far as I go
That shit overseas
don't really affect me

It's World War III
civil war in a pop-top can
Fat people
with skinny souls
And no one cares
'cause if they did
things would change
Elected
only to neglect
the ones who put them there

But who am I to criticize
it's double-talk
I realize
if I'm not part of the solution
I'm part of the problem
So,
who's gonna solve it all
Maybe the end is near
ignorance is bliss
Pucker up
for one last kiss

Where

Where have all the white sprinters gone
Where have all the black swimmers gone
Wish I knew
Hell,
for all we know
they could be right in front of you
A wise man
ain't that wise
if he don't open his eyes
A blind man
ain't that blind
if he listens with an open mind

How did it go so wrong
How did it all get twisted
We go forward in reverse
We make it better
just to make it worse
Guess we're only as smart
as the knowledge we seek
'Cause the black swimmer is here
and the white sprinter
never went anywhere

Blue

It's the end
and what did I do
I hit that wall
but never got through
How will they remember me
How will they remember you
Did I touch your life
Were you a good husband
Were you a good wife
Is the world a better place
Are you a better person
Questions will pass
from me to you
and to the next
until the ground is full
of the passions and desires
that never made it through
overflowing with the dreams that faded
and the dark skies
that never turned blue

Big cities
with their big problems
politicians
unwilling to solve them
A crook with wings
made away with everything
And the cycle continues
as we all turn our heads
point the finger at the next man
tell him who should sleep in his bed
War planes fly mach 3
Will they remember you
Will they remember me
There's a hole in the bottom

and it's filled to the brim
More people and more hopeless
falling deeper and deeper within
The cycle continues
from the touch to the taste
the gluttony to the waste
What did we change
What did we really change

Gone

Where do I run
Where do I hide
when it's me
I don't want to find
The truth hurts
when it forces you to change
when you realize your ignorance
has kept you the same
I've got a pocket full of ambition
but a mind full of doubt
To live with
or to live without
To fade away
or burn out
I walk the streets
looking for yesterday
wrapped within tonight
I know it's in vain
but I look anyway
The life I had is gone
but tonight I'll play the songs of my past
and try to go back
I'll light the candle
the scent that burned long ago
But the moment is gone
Yesterday is gone

Conform

No one knows
what food will make their garden grow
There are no daisies
no roses
no tulips in my yard
no sunshine behind the clouds
no regret
from their disregard
Who shall I be
What color shall I force my eyes to see
Complete,
yet unknowing
I was blind
I searched for the truth they told me to find
I conformed to their ways
I was the mouse
in their distorted maze
Ripped and torn
eventually the new me was born
an angel bent and twisted
into the devil's form
Wasting one heart after another
betraying my soul
with a host of nameless lovers
Broken and bent
they stole my innocence
I conformed to their ways
I was the monkey
dancing in their cage
Trapped
like so many good souls before me
in their evil
Conformity

Scars

Can you be my saving grace
Can you help me save face
Been a lot and a little
to a lot of different people
but never found the high
to equal me out

Do you believe in God
Do you trust the stars
Do you think Jesus
can heal my scars

I'm looking for hope
in all the wrong places
I'm looking for hope
through a broken telescope
It's pointed to the heavens
but all I see
is a cracked and blurred
reflection of me

Do you believe in God
Do you trust the stars
Do you think Jesus
can forgive my scars

Samantha

They call her Samantha,
Listener of God
But I'd give anything
if she'd listen to me
if she'd listen to the world
If Samantha could talk back
what would she say
what would He do

Samantha,
what do you hear
when your ear is to the sky
What do you feel
when God touches you on the inside
I pray
but where do my words go
I've said too much
and done too little
for God to give a shit about me

Samantha,
will you tell me
what God sounds like
Is His voice sweet and pure
Does it give you the strength to endure
another disappointing day
another hard-learned mistake
Does His love ring out
Does His warmth remove all your doubts
They call her Samantha,
Listener of God
But I'd give anything
if she'd listen to me
I'd give anything
if He'd listen to the world

Hell

I want to burn in hell
like the lost souls before me
If God can start the fire
then heaven is the kingdom
I refuse to admire
If God exists
I hope He loves us all
as much when we rise
as when we fall
Life can be a living hell
A reality too many
know too well
If Your love
can burn my soul
Then hell
is where I want to go
And when God asks why I didn't follow
it's 'cause my friendships
I didn't borrow
I'll join those
that passed before me
The ones who didn't know You so well
The ones my preacher says
are burning in hell

WAR

This is an introduction to WAR!
To inhumanity's greatest form
To futility at its peak
Who will stand and fight
for the rights of those sent off to war
Is it freedom or oil
need or greed
It's the ghost of McCarthy
come back from the dead
Hunting
Searching
for the connection that isn't there
Where are the witches
with their broomsticks and ballistic missiles
With war comes victory and defeat
With life comes compassion and truth
This is an introduction to war
a salute to those on foreign soil
to the innocent fighting in a rich man's war

If there's a God
please shine your light on me
and my enemies
Darkness falls
and death isn't far behind
I've been sent to kill
someone I don't even know
Save my soul,
for I only do what I'm told
And I'm trying so hard
to make sense of it all
Sometimes standing
is as painful as the fall

Death fills the air

Burning souls rip holes in my psyche
I breathe in pain
my soul stained
my life rearranged
Horror and guilt
etched on my heart and mind
What I saw in the desert
I'll never leave behind
Did we really have to do this
Did we really have to go to War

Never knew life could get this bad
Never knew a mother's face could look so sad
Tears fall on the desert sand
They say the scars made me a man
but I'd give it all back
to be innocent and young
not the unsung hero
not the man who knows
what I know
Death and life intertwined
I try to rewind
Now my life is confined
to the horrors locked within my mind

3
<u>BUT LOVE WON ME OVER</u>

Without hope,
all we have is yesterday

Destination

I want to love you
like death loves life
I want to taste the worst part of you
and make it sweet
The deepest words can't fathom
The strongest hands can't hold
what I have for you

Too often
we fail to express
the best of what we have to offer
But in this moment
everything I have
I've spent
everything I owned
I gave
'cause you are the cure
for a life less-lived
You make everything I've ever done
worth it

All the hits
All the misses
All the regret,
landed me next to you
I've second-guessed
lost faith
and all the while,
someone was steering my ship in your direction
My journey
was worth the destination

Space

In our infinite smallness
I felt grand with you in my arms
A star in the heavens
only shines as bright
as the eyes that can see it
Love is space
and time
often helps us find
what we're looking for

I've been to the desert
in search of water
been given the path to love
only to falter
crafted the perfect ring
only to be left at the alter
Love ain't always kind
but if God is on my side
who can oppose me
If He places you in my arms
who can take you away
In our infinite smallness
I felt God
with you in my arms

<u>Rush</u>

Sometimes I fall
just to feel the rush
Sometimes I fall
just to get back up
'Cause there's nothing like a crush
even if it's made up
To taste,
is to live
To love,
is to give
Though I know you're wrong
I want to belong
Though I know it will hurt in the end
I want to give in
'Cause weakness starts in the heart
then travels to the mind
Sometimes I fall
simply for the touch
Sometimes I fall
'cause I'm not strong enough
to say no

Eager

What will it take
to make you mine
We got this long distance thing
but I'm more of a sprinter
caught between the warmth of summer
and the cold of winter

Never seen a hand I couldn't hold
Never been a fan of self-control
But now
something's changed
You make me
want to slow it all down

Through a telephone line
your soul warms the cold in me
The new moon shines
through the slats in my window blinds
Funny to think,
you can see the same damn thing

The phone line connects us
The moonlight resurrects us
What I thought I'd lost
I've found
Confirmed by what we tried to deny
a moment in the dark
renewed our spark

Hope

I'm holding out
holding on
to something bigger than me
I'm so small
and she's so tall
Alone we have nothing
but together
we have it all

I'm a little neurotic at times
not O-C-D,
just a little self-indulgent
See,
I'm an only child
and been single most of my life
I've built my walls
I won't deny
Kind of over the top
Not used to having it all
but still demand a lot
Hot and cold
some days who knows
But I'll try
to self-medicate
for the sake of us
'Cause love
is the cure for my disease
and I think you
are the perfect remedy

I know you've been hurt before
seen the pain in your eyes
Yeah,
you're too honest to deny
too open to hide

the scars on the inside
I'll let you think
you pulled one over on me
but I can see
that you're into me
And you'd be a fool
if you didn't see
how much I'm into you

I'm a little neurotic at times
a little more into the dream
than reality
My last crush
was pretty much all made up
I was tired
so tired of being alone
Guess that only child thing
wore off years ago
I'm a little neurotic ya see
but I guess
a little less than I used to be
So I'll try
to self-medicate
for the sake of us
'Cause love
is the cure for my disease
and you
are my perfect remedy

Key

It's the first week of winter
and I'm freezing
tired of love teasing
ready to start seeing
what you're really all about
We dance and we laugh
A wink and a smile
at the most random of times
Even in the midst of our winter
our sun found a way to shine
If love is a jury
then you are my trial
and I can't deny
I'm guilty
honest to God I'm guilty
of opening the gates
and letting your wave rush over me

Piano keys
echo through the room
a warm June breeze
on a December afternoon
Reverb
looking for a noun
for someone to love
in between the descriptive words
a touch that lasts into the morning
and offers the truth
even when it doesn't have to

Guitar strings
sing to the heavens
a solo
looking for a partner
We fall

and our autumn's finally come
A love born
from a love on the run
And less is more
for someone like me
Your voice
was the perfect pitch
the key
to unlocking me

She

She
was like a bolt of lightening from the darkest sky
She rained her light
on everything
and anything around

She
couldn't have been built better in my mind
To the beat of her own drum
she sings her song
and I hum along

She
comes with no strings
and I'm so attached
to the fact
that She never holds back

She
keeps coming
Intellectually stunning
So much more
than the most curious mind
could ever explore

She
compensates for my mistakes
She renegotiates her take
and all I can do
is thank God I found you

Supernova

There's life
death,
and somewhere in between
A black hole of gravity
tugging at our souls
We may not see the light
but we know the end
is on the other side
So we fight
we scrap
we brawl with the will of our future
and the hope
that what we dream
survives

I've come from the depths
of darkness and beyond
felt the loneliness of space
but carried on
A supernova
who left the heavens behind
for this fleeting thing
we call love
For life may be short
but it burns so bright
So bright
a star would give up it's stellar light
to seek out a heavenly love
in an earthly life

IT BEGAN…

4
UNTIL MY MIND WAS OPENED

I conjure up the demons in my mind
If God won't help me,
who will?
I've never been above honesty
So if the best in me,
is the worst in me
so be it

Sad Song

I had a friend
we don't talk much anymore
It's not my fault
and I don't blame him
Time has a way
of making even the brightest lights dim
Alone on the floor
I cry as the song rolls along
Guess my mother was right
even the best of friends
don't always belong

I went back
to the place I once called home
I've never felt so alone
the lights that shone on me
had long since faded
and all traces of me
all negated
Alone on the floor
I cry as the song rolls along
Guess my mother was right
every good memory
turns into a sad,
sad song

Now I know why she doesn't listen
to her records anymore
She doesn't want to feel
all she's lost
She knew one day
I'd understand her ways
So I sit in silence
afraid of what I've left behind
I don't want to listen

I don't want the music to find
the memories lost to time
the lives
no longer a part of mine

No Man's Land

I exist
on a plateau before God
on a hillside near heaven
on the edge of a kingdom
built to birth a landslide
For the heights of my spirit
can only soar for so long
A desperate captain
steering his ship into no man's land
A fearless soldier
fighting in my first and last war
A pawn sent into battle
though I don't know what I'm fighting for
I roam
I flee
I start
I stop
fell to the bottom
then climbed 'til I reached the top
all to realize
I was still lost
Inhale…

I yearned for insight
searched for the light
And finally
on the darkest of nights
I looked to the sky
and the moon brought me home
Though peace eludes me
the breeze sets me free
the sun opens my sails
and the wind carries me
I exist
on a plateau before God

on a hillside near heaven
on the edge of a kingdom
built to birth a landslide
Exhale...

E

There's not much left
'cause I gave it all away
In a wave of generosity
I gave you the best of me

Runnin' on E
has become a daily necessity
Runnin' on e
has come to redefine me

How does one rebound
from the sound of silence
How does one find a reason
to end the grieving season

Runnin' on E
has become a daily necessity
Runnin' on e
has come to define me

<u>Bend</u>

What do you say
when everything's been said
Where do you put your soul
when the conflict's in your head

I wish I could set aside
a warm place to hide
a disguise
to mask what I can no longer deny

I can feel it creeping in
that bend in the road
and I'm turning on the inside
trying to set aside my pride
'cause the best things in life
seem to happen
when you give in

Resistance

A picture in a frame
with no wall to hang her heart on
From state to state
From soul to soul
She's a change in the weather
I can't control
And when it rains it pours
and I think I adore
you
All you are
All you were
And all that you'll become
If resistance is the key
then this door is not for me
My willpower's gone
eroded by the years
Too many of Cupid's spears
have had their way with me

Beautiful

Pretty girls
I thought I'd learned
the hotter they are
the more they burn
You could've had me
but you walked away
There was no room for us
in your little dream world
I was a distraction
on your path to perfection
just another casualty
on the way to your destination

Burned
another lesson learned
A night in the life
of a moon that hung too high
A starry-eyed smile
I was living in denial
Too much for the truth
You were too much for me
Your eyes for tomorrow
could never see today
I wanted to believe
in all we could be
But you walked away
in love
with your little dream world

Inspired?

Have I built you up in my mind
or am I just longing to find
something
or someone
to fill the void
Am I lonely or inspired
ignorant or tired
Am I enthusiastic
or in denial
I've compiled quite a resume
a list of letdowns,
yeah,
I think I've heard it all before
I'm fading fast
alas,
I've come too far
to go back home
So tired
So damn tired
of being alone
Am I lonely or inspired
ignorant or tired
Maybe
I'm just in love

July

It's a telephone call
when the tears are scattered on the floor
In the void of night
when loneliness weighs the heaviest
Life's a recurring dream
that never stops
The rain falls
and I call
another dead-end soul
Something inside of me
just can't let go
A voice I hardly recognize
A passion I've long since forgotten
Hello's as good as goodbye
'cause nothing lasts forever
except the void of night

Wake

There are angels in my dust
laying in my wake
So still and so honest
If the truth were told
If the lies were all dispersed
I would be the victim!
I would be the fool!
For running so fast
in this fast-paced world
For tuning out tomorrow
when I focused on today
There are angels in my wake
and I'm lying to myself
There are angels in my wake
and I'm laying in my dust

Undone

I'm done
I'm so done
I had my day in the sun
All has turned to none
Neatly fitted
just came undone
The lights flashed
and the sirens roared
I could only cry
as they closed the doors
I knew I'd see my friend no more
I'm done
I'm so Undone

Chelsea

She met a boy
the day before me
He filled her with blanks
bullets of naivety
Needles
Shiny things
and everything in between
Chelsea was a beauty queen
Chelsea was the talk of the town
she was the most honest thing
I'd ever seen
Now Chelsea,
ain't really that Chelsea anymore
Wish I could go back
and conjure up the past
But all good things
can't always last
I pray the chains of what happened
can one day be unfastened

Why do nice girls
find the baddest boys
They get a wild ride
then get tossed aside
Chelsea,
if I could steal one minute
we could live an entire lifetime in it
We could go back
to the last day of your youth
save your innocence
and protect you from you
So full of promise
So full of life
Oh,
what could have been

before the devil crept in
Before you became a slave
to the insecurities within
Oh Chelsea,
if only we could go back

Cut

She cuts herself
to stay alive
She doesn't deny
what she's become
'cause she's finally becoming
who she really is
What will it take
to break the chains
what will it take
for her to regain
the cut

She makes the most of the day
She paints pictures in her mind,
of the end
One swerve
One leap
One swallow
The cut runs deep
'cause to her
half dead
is better than half alive

Close

Last night we were close
but somehow close,
is never close enough
We sat
as people with secrets often do
Alone yet together
innocent yet vile
Guess we're all a little messed up inside
some of us just have a better place to hide
So I ponder each twist
each turn
each hill and valley in my mind
Tonight I'll ponder simple things
little things
all the things
we could have been

Perfect

I'm the sun
in the middle of the sky
I touch the world
but no one touches me

I'm a leaf
dangling from a branch
dreaming of a windy day
when the breeze starts to blow
and I'm forced to let go

I'm a shadow in the dark
that no one can see
waiting for a light
to expose my true identity

I'm a rock in a stream
that flows night and day
Though I feel the cool embrace
with every touch
I erode away

I'm a mirror that fails to reflect
I'm the place where love and hate intersect
The voice of an angel
singing to an empty crowd
Perfect in my imperfection
An unforgettable smile
Followed by an awkward hesitation
So much for having it all
So much for perfection
hiding our flaws

5
<u>TO ALL THAT WAS</u>

She was a corner
I had to turn

For You

I'm not the best to everyone
not a hero to all
But for you,
I want to be the silver lining
'Cause there's nothing better
than being better
than the past
And I don't know if I ever said it
though I should have a long time ago

No one gets there alone
No one owns
a life all their own
We all need a helping hand
somewhere safe to land
Sometimes I wonder what could have been
but the waves wash it all away
the good
and the bad
but I'm glad to have
what we had
'Cause no one gets there alone
And I don't know if I ever said it
though I should have a long time ago
thank you

Habit

I'm breakin' the habit
of not breakin' through
killin' the curse
that was passed to me from you
A gift in the wind
blowing in the breeze
and it's up to me
to set it free
I dream
only to awake in worse shape
I run
but can't escape
Fallin'
Stallin'
Time to stop complaining
and go all in

Without

We were broken
from the very beginning
From the rise of our first sun
to it's first dimming
We clung to hope
even when doubt crept in
I mean
what were we supposed to do
We wanted us so damn bad
We ignored our truth
until we couldn't anymore
Deliberate
We finally sank the ship we came in on
We raised the white flag
but my heart carried on
I prayed for the day
when faith would be rewarded
and love granted
and we could be
without resistance

Sometimes

Sometimes
it takes a fall to inspire the flight
Sometimes
you have to do it wrong
to get it right
The future baffles me
almost as much as the past
but I'm here
and that's all that really matters, right?
I talk to angels
make deals with devils
Sometimes
it takes a little bit of both
Yeah
you know it's true

Used to look to the future
Now I'm smack dab in the middle of it
Ain't getting any younger
but that's okay
I'm ready for a new outlook anyway
Been living in and out of two worlds
One hand reaching through heaven's floor
One foot propping open the devil's door
Can't seem to find my place
in the big picture
A promise
covered in doubt
The only way in
is the only way out
I talk to angels
make deals with devils
And I wouldn't have it any other way
It takes a little bit of both,
to get it right

Sifting

I'm sifting through
what's left of my life
Gonna put it in a bottle
and let the ocean decide
Will it make the shore
or rest on the ocean floor

I rode a wave
that brought me to the world
saw the chaos
and climbed back on my board
I could've tried to spark a change,
but what for
No one listens
too many distractions
to take action
Too many painkillers
to feel any real passion

A paradox
Life locks you in
It's hard to be good
but so easy to sin
A passion in progress
A total beauty
A total mess
Life is love
Love is theft
I rode a wave
that brought me to the shore
I got a handful of nothing
but still wanted more

Time

Who am I
but the pieces I've broken
Who am I
but the pieces I've picked up
Alive in a million different ways
What decays
makes a brilliant return one day
A life torn
is stitched up
and takes on a new form
Embrace the pain
Find peace in the change
In the end
all you have
is all you put in
Shine for you
Shine for me
Give your all
to all your beliefs
From time to time
we look to the sky
Be the light
that brings hope to someone's night
Be the hope
shining through someone else's
long range telescope

Save

I search for inspiration
mental stimulation
intellectual penetration
a Godly vibration
Glorious
is the one who saves
Immortal
is the one who paves the way
Salvage a life gone bad
Give hope
Give everything you have
We live
then we die
But between your day and night
Save someone else's life

Drive

Drive
Hit the gas 'til you feel alive
We've only one life to live
You gotta give it all you got
Don't milk the clock
Go long
Take the big shot
Ride the wave
'til you hit the shore
Give it all you got
then give a little more
Live long
Die fast
Live your first
like it's your last
I woke up and hit the gas
checked my rearview
then vowed to never look back
I embarked at sunrise
I'll drive 'til my sky turns black
I'll drive
'til I feel alive

IT BEGAN…

6
AND ALL THAT WASN'T

I was born for tomorrow
but I'm here today
I was born to shine
but I'm fading away

Fire

We wage war
Make babies
Love and kill
Build just to break
Give just to take
We steal time like it's ours to make
We conquer the skies
just to escape
what we built on the ground
Selfish,
yet generous
A little bit of good
and bad in all of us
We burn 'til we flame out
But where does our fire go
when the smoke fades away
Are we
all that we are
The past is written
and quoted through time
But I can't hold it
can't control it
I got nothin'
but this fire within
So I ask,
when the time we stole catches up to us
where does our fire go?

<u>Lovely</u>

I got her picture
on the front of my phone
She's got her belly
in the palm of her hands
It's growin'
Pretty soon she'll be showin'
thanks to some magician
who came
then disappeared
as the big day neared

But she's so lovely
and she's starting to see
everything her life
is supposed to be
She's rising above
the waves crashing at her door
She's destined to be more
'cause she's starting to understand
what God put her here for

She ain't gotta run no more
She ain't gotta regret a Goddamn thing
The movement in her
moves her soul
Now the power inside
gives her control
of a life she never knew she had
It's the 21st
and life could be a whole lot worse
17 days
'til she gives her old life away
And she's so lovely
to me

Two Years

I gave two years and 17 days
only to watch what I fought for
crumble
and fade away
I gave the best of me
to a person who didn't deserve it
Now I'm stuck
standing in the rain
under the dark clouds
and the numbing pain
listening to the sound of nothing
grow louder

But are my problems
really problems
Some might say
they're distractions
getting in the way
A million little girls
won't eat today
A million little boys
don't have a home
Millions of lost souls
out there all alone

I wake up
while millions never went to sleep
I eat
while millions of mothers grieve
And here I sit
sipping coffee and surfing the internet
The sad thing is
I don't really regret
not making a difference
I stare at the girl behind the counter

and wonder how she tastes
I could really care less
about the rest of the human race
'Cause if I really gave a shit
I'd get over me
and do something to fix it

Bagel

He died
but to her,
he's still alive
He's gone
but been with her all along
We see
the hurt in her eyes
but in his absence
she doesn't cry
she just gives her all
as if he was still alive

What's the point
in letting reality slow you down
Rules were meant to bend
and she's doing her best
to break the law
'Cause she can't imagine
a life without him
They met in high school
She played the nerd
he played the fool
goofing around
just to calm himself down
A first kiss
and 16 years of bliss
She's only 32
what's she going to do
with the memory
of a man
she can't be next to

A bagel
with coffee and cream
She takes a bite

then starts to daydream
Alone in a café
he walks through the door
she squeezes him with everything
she wants nothing more
But his image quickly fades
and reality sinks in
She lost the love of her life
her best friend

Time moves on
and one day so will she
She's alone
but not free
They met in high school
She played it tough
she played it cool
He played the jock
he played the tool
A life is gone
and she knows
there's nothing she can do
but eat her bagel
and try to find her dream in the day
Her lost love
is her escape

Inside

She walked
from the café to the bar
after making a quick stop
back at her car
A drink from a flask
and a drag from her last cigarette
Now her belly is warm
but her heart still cold
The ice from old scars
won't let her
let go

She's meeting some girls
she met on New Year's Eve
After 2 years
she's back on the scene
trying to find
something to redeem
her belief in love
She wants a boy who can talk
about life and the world
not a typical guy
searching for the next easy girl

The winter breeze
tells her it's time to go inside
Her body may be cold
but her soul is warm
The ashes of her past
float into the sky
and she can no longer deny
she's ready to see love
in a new pair of eyes

<u>You</u>

I listen
to the songs we used to play
I eat the food
we tried at that one place
down the road
But it don't taste the same
It don't feel the same
without you
I walk
down the streets
of the old neighborhood
but the sky ain't as pretty
and the breeze don't feel as good
I wish it would
God I wish it could

How long
will I think about you
Guess it's about time
I think about replacing you
But the truth is
I still miss you
even though I wonder
if I ever really knew you
Maybe I never did
Maybe I crafted you in my mind
But whatever you are
or whoever you were
I still miss you
And whatever we had
or didn't have
I still miss the good
I still miss the bad
How long
will it take to get over you

the girl I loved,
but never really knew

<u>Walk</u>

When did you know
When did you realize
the love of your life
wasn't the one by your side
It hurt
It hurt so bad
'cause you know deep down
they gave you all they had
Now you gotta walk
away from
the only one
who ever gave you a shot

Do you sit up
at all hours of the night
trying to figure it out
trying to make it right
Sometimes
it just is what it is
In time
maybe they'll forgive you
Maybe in time
they'll thank you

For once,
someone didn't leave you stranded
They held your hand
and made you part of their plan
You'd always been the one
people walked away from
You always wanted
someone to stick around
Now you finally found
someone to stay
And now you're the one

ready to walk away

Can't love
if the spark ain't there
Can't rearrange your emotions
it wouldn't be fair
Do you stick around
tell your heart to be quiet
give it that hush sound
tell it to keep walking
with its head down
There's no easy way
to walk away
No easy way
to give away
all they gave to you
But you gotta walk
if you know
the love by your side
ain't the love of your life

Friend

They come and go
in and out of our lives
The people who inspire
the world in us
They make us laugh
They make us cry
'Cause we
can't go it alone
How many people
crossed your path
How many best friends
promised forever
but didn't last
Life is long
but love is short
I sit here
wishing I had a little more
from so many
who walked through my door
Am I naïve
to believe
I'll get a second chance
Am I naïve
to believe
I haven't seen the last of you

Together

I've cried
on the happiest of nights
afraid to lose
the woman by my side
She's been there
since day number 1
9 months before
I was even born
She carried me then
and carries me now
A single mom
She did it on her own
And who am I
but the man she made of me
Her glue
keeps me from breaking apart
I got her honesty
I got her heart
The most moral person I know
though she shows
so little sometimes
Been hardened by the years
Maybe it's the fear
of losing what she has left
She's cried
on the happiest of nights
afraid to lose
what she has by her side
Her friends are getting older
and the thought hovers over her
How much longer
can she be the strong one
I wonder
if she really knows
how much people truly love her

It Began

It Began So Innocently
through the sapphire
and crimson lives
we shattered with the breath of our intentions
Fearless
We owned the world
in spite of the night

Then Thought Crept In
devouring with wrath
our most honest mines
A barrier of youth
hobbled by our faith
in all we believed,
that wasn't

But Love Won Me Over
In a flash of light
a beam of honesty
a stream of warmth
a want my heart had never possessed
And I was possessed
unafraid of the remains
history laid at my feet
Despite the logical end
I bought in

Until My Mind Was Opened
to the pain in you
the loss of you
the past
I could never erase
the present
I could never hold
the future

I could never own
I told myself
one day none of this will matter
But despite my doubts
my heart relented

To All That Was
to come
Fight or flight
Seize or release
The moment is ours to take
Youth verses age
Love verses hate
We must find a way
to turn the page

And All That Wasn't
isn't all that's meant to be
The wrecking ball
comes from upon high
The vengeance of all
we should have been
But fuck it
If we all end in nothing
everything we own
is ours to give
When our last seconds tick into oblivion
we can still live on
in the fires we lit along the way
Blessed,
because we offered our best
to those with less
We begin
to end
that longing
lacking
sadness of the world.

PAUL GIVENS

ABOUT THE AUTHOR

Paul Givens was raised in Muskogee, Oklahoma. He currently lives in Minneapolis, where the extreme seasons and hipster coffee shops feed his creative spirit.

PAUL GIVENS